GREAT SMOKY
MOUNTAINS

NATIONAL PARK

by Ruth Radlauer

Design and photographs by Rolf Zillmer

AN ELK GROVE BOOK

 CHILDRENS PRESS ™

CHICAGO

With gratitude to the people of
Tennessee and North Carolina, and
special thanks to the Park Rangers
and Volunteers in the Park.

National Park Service Photographs by
Clair Burket, Great Smoky Mountains
National Park on pages 21, 36, and
38. Page 33, National Park Service.

Cover: Cades Cove

Library of Congress Cataloging in Publication Data

Radlauer, Ruth Shaw.
  Great Smoky Mountains National Park.

  (Parks for people)
  "An Elk Grove book."
  SUMMARY: Introduces the many enjoyments to be found
in Great Smoky Mountains National Park, located in
Tennessee and North Carolina.
  1. Great Smoky Mountains National Park—Juvenile
literature. [1. Great Smoky Mountains National Park.
2. National parks and reserves] I. Zillmer, Rolf.
II. Title.
F443.G7R3   917.68'89   76-9839
ISBN 0-516-07489-X

5 6 7 8 9 10 11 12 13 14 15 R 91 90 89 88 87 86 85

Contents

Great Smoky Mountains National Park

Miles and miles of streams and hiking trails. That's what Great Smoky Mountains National Park is. It's the rushing sound of waterfalls and the quiet of a hardwood forest.

This park is the smell of hamburgers cooking over a smoky wood fire at the Elkmont Campground.

The Smokies are high mountain peaks like Mount Le Conte and Chimney Tops. They're wide, peaceful valleys where you can see houses and barns the early settlers built. You can even visit a farm and talk with the farmer's wife as she cooks on the fireplace hearth.

Your national park is a paradise for backpacking, birdwatching, and wildflower photography. It's a wealth of fishing streams and nature trails.

Great Smoky Mountains National Park is a place to be with people who love trees and flowers, birds and blue skies as much as you do. Or it's a place to be quiet and wonder about all the things that live here.

Miles Of Streams

Elkmont Campground

Chimney Tops

Pioneer Farmstead—Oconaluftee

She Cooks On The Hearth

How to Enjoy the Park

The Great Smoky Mountains are part of the Appalachian Mountain Range. This range of mountains reaches from Maine to Georgia. In the park, the crest of the Appalachians runs between Tennessee and North Carolina.

In Tennessee, you enter the park from Gatlinburg or Townsend. North Carolina entrances are at Cherokee and Bryson City.

You'll enjoy the park more if you go to one of the Visitor Centers first. At Oconaluftee, North Carolina, there are pictures and displays that show places to go and things to do in the Smokies. Nearby you can visit a farm and watch a farmer and his wife as they work the same way early settlers did.

In the Visitor Center at Sugarlands, Tennessee, exhibits explain many of the plants and animals in the park. Ranger talks and nature walks go on here as well as at other centers and campgrounds.

All visitor centers have post cards, books, free maps, and visitor programs. If you want to camp overnight in the backcountry, you get your permit at any visitor center.

For a map and other information write, Superintendent, Great Smoky Mountains National Park, Gatlinburg, TN 37738.

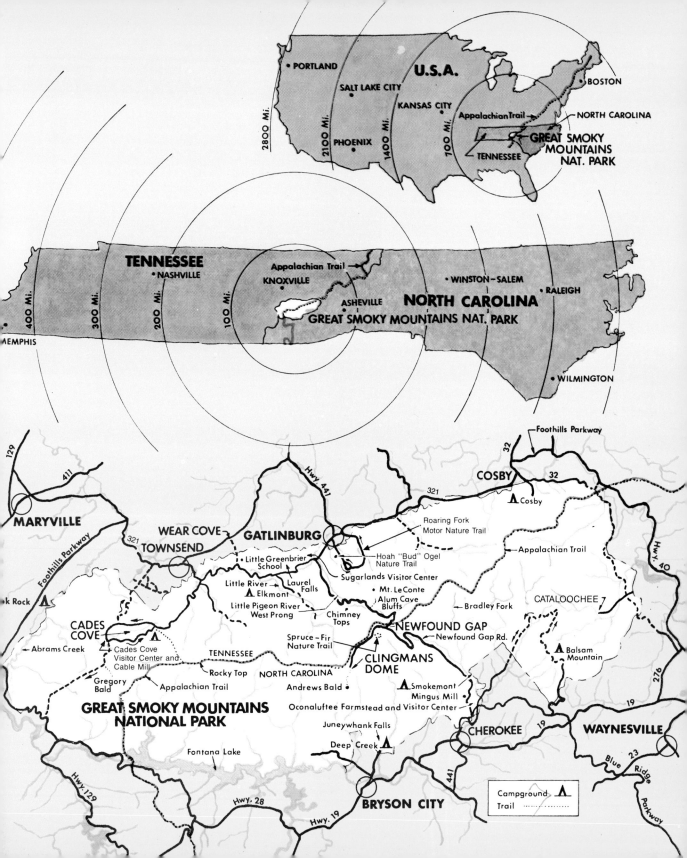

Why Smokies?

When you visit these mountains, you'll see why they're called the Smokies. Millions of trees and shrubs give off water vapor and oil. Tiny drops of vapor and oil floating in the air make a smoke or haze that clings to the peaks. You can find haze in other mountains, but it's thicker here because of heavy rainfall and many trees.

As you travel up the mountains you find many different kinds of plants. At the lowest elevations, near Abrams Creek, are plants like the sweet gum tree that like warm temperatures. Higher up you find oaks, hemlock, and maples. At the highest elevations, mountain ash, fir, red spruce, and other plants grow well in cold temperatures.

If you climb one of the trails to Mount Le Conte, you'll see how plant life changes as temperatures change. And you'll know why the Indians called these mountains "Shagonigei" (Shah go nee gay ee), or "like blue smoke."

Many Elevations—Many Kinds Of Trees

A Visit to the Past

The Smokies and the river valleys around them were once the home of the Cherokee Indians. But settlers, hungry for freedom and land, began to crowd into the mountains and valleys. The Cherokees tried to keep their home. Sometimes they fought. Other times they made treaties. Finally the U.S. Army took charge of thousands of Cherokees and moved them to Oklahoma, then known as Indian Territory. Along the way 4000 Indians died. This route is now called the "Trail of Tears."

A visit to Cades Cove or the Farmstead at Oconaluftee can be a visit to the settlers' past. At Oconaluftee, a farmer and his wife go about the work of the farm. When you look into the kitchen, you may find a woman baking cornbread on the hearth or churning butter in the sunlight by the door.

Outside, a bunch of geese go honking past the apple house. The farmer may be feeding the pig or repairing a wagon. You can almost feel how it was to live here long ago.

Butter Churning—Oconaluftee

Geese By The Apple House

To Hew a Home

Melting snow and rain carry soil, plants, and rocks down a mountain. The soil and plants build a rich, gentle slope called a cove.

Early settlers in the Smokies found many rich, sloping coves. They were happy to find chestnut trees and tall, straight yellow poplar trees to build houses, barns, and other farm buildings.

Using pole axes and wooden wedges called gluts, they split the poplars in half, then split those halves in half again.

They smoothed, or hewed, the flat sides of the logs with broad axes and draw knives. The hewed poplar made thick, wide wooden planks for the house walls.

Sometimes the settlers placed the corners of houses on rocks already sitting in the ground. Other times they piled up rocks and made sure the corners were truly square. They notched the planks at the ends to make chamfer notch corners. Because of their careful work, many of these early homes still stand today.

John Oliver's House, The First In Cades Cove

Chamfer Notch Corner

With a Roof to Cover Their Heads

When you visit this park, be sure to spend a long time at Cades Cove where some of the first settlers built their homes. Here you may see a man making shingles for a roof.

Mountain folk believe that a tree for shingles must be cut down "on the dark side of the moon," the time between full moon and new moon. They say, "If you cut your tree on the wrong side of the moon, the shingles will curl."

Shingles are split with a wooden mallet and a tool called a froe. Starting with a two-foot piece of oak, a person holds the froe at the end of the wood and hits the froe with the mallet. As the wood splits, he works the froe down through the wood until the whole piece is split apart. Then he splits the pieces again until the shingles are about half an inch thick.

Laid on the roof, the shingles protect the inside from sun and rain. When it rains, the shingles swell and fit together more tightly to keep out the rain.

Hit The Froe With A Mallet

Split The Oak With The Froe

Lay Shingles On The Roof This Way

And Food on the Table

With no stores for miles around, the settlers had to hunt and raise their own food. Corn was the main crop. People ate it fresh or dried and ground into cornmeal.

Some farms had mills to grind the corn. Many streams rushing down the mountainside gave power to turn the mills. Today water power turns turbine wheels like the tub mill at the Noah "Bud" Ogle Place. Water power also turns an overshot wheel like John Cable's at Cades Cove. As water falls over it, the wheel turns. The overshot wheel turns a set of gears that turn a round, flat stone. The turning stone sits on another flat stone and grinds corn between the two.

Near Oconaluftee, you can visit the Mingus Mill where a turbine wheel powers the grinder.

At Mingus Mill and John Cable's Mill, you can buy cornmeal for baking good things to eat.

John Cable's Mill—Cades Cove

The Overshot Wheel—Cades Cove

Tub Mill Turbine

Cornmeal For Sale

Sweetening

The farm women made cornbread, and cornbread needs butter and sweetening. Some farms had a cow for milk to make butter. For sweetening people made sugar from sugar maple trees. They also used honey and sorghum molasses.

To get honey, people smoked bees out of their hives in hollow trees. Or they moved a swarm to a hollow black gum log with holes in the bottom. The bees made a new hive in this "bee gum" and people gathered the honey.

For sorghum molasses, people grew sorghum cane. This grass-like plant has a stalk with a soft center full of sweet juice. Horse or ox-power turned rollers in a sorghum mill. The rollers squeezed the juice out of the stalks.

People came from all around to help when the juice was boiled in a big flat pan over a stone furnace. They told stories, laughed, and sang while the juice boiled down into a thick syrup. The golden or dark brown syrup was called "long sweetenin' " or molasses.

Bee Gum Stand—Oconaluftee

Sorghum Mill—Oconaluftee

A Big Flat Pan For Boiling Sorghum Juice

Animals

At first people hunted deer, wild turkeys, bears, and other animals. But soon most of the deer were gone and bears hid in the high country.

In the 1880s there were many wild turkeys. A few years later, they were almost gone. People said the wild turkeys would soon be extinct.

This did not happen. Some wild turkeys lived on. But even with protection, there are not many turkeys in the park today. Animals like skunks, opossums, hawks, and snakes eat turkey eggs and young chicks.

Wild turkeys used to eat acorns, beechnuts, and chestnuts. Today, the American chestnut tree has been killed off by a sickness, or blight, and that means turkeys have less food.

If you are lucky, you'll see some wild turkeys in Cades Cove at the edge of a meadow or in open fields. Of the many kinds of animals in the park, 22 species are salamanders. There are about 60 kinds of mammals, and over 200 kinds of birds.

Wild Turkeys

Striped Skunk

Clothing

In Cades Cove you can visit the first frame house built in the Smokies, the Becky Cable house. Here you may see a loom like the ones used to weave cloth for dresses, shirts, and pants.

Becky Cable may have grown cotton to make thread or sheared a sheep for wool. First she had to wash dirt and some of the oil out of the wool. Then, with flat wire brushes called carders, she combed the hairs of wool and made them into a roll. She used a spinning wheel or hand spindle to spin the roll into yarn for the loom.

Women made their own soap for washing. To get lye for soap they put ashes from the fireplace in a wooden bin, an ash hopper. By running water over the hopper, they soaked a brown liquid full of lye out of the ashes. This liquid, boiled with several pounds of animal fat, made a thick, jelly-like soap that hardened enough to cut into bars. Even today, many mountain people make their own soap.

A Loom At Becky Cable's House—Cades Cove ►

Little Greenbrier School

Many of the earliest settlers had gone to school before they came to the Smoky Mountains. But life in the Smokies was hard. Parents had little time to teach children to read and write.

From their mothers, girls learned to weave, bake, and keep a garden. Boys helped their fathers hunt and plow. These were the only lessons the young people had. When children grew up and had families, their children did not learn to read or write, either.

The day came when very few people in the Smokies could read or write. It was time to build a school. Families got together and built the Little Greenbrier School. At first its one big room had benches but no tables or desks. A big stove sat in the middle of the room to warm 50 to 70 children.

Today you can visit this school. From Sugarlands, drive along the Little River Road to Metcalf Bottoms. Then take the road toward Wear Cove. After you walk to the school, you can listen as the teacher tells what it was like to go to a one-room school.

Little Greenbrier School Built In 1882 ►

A Lantern to Find the Way

Girls and boys went to the new school for only three months a year. The rest of the year they had to help with planting and harvesting.

The teacher's pay was 35¢ a day plus food and a place to live. Later there was more money for schools, and state law said schools must stay open eight months a year.

Some children walked almost four miles to school. They left home very early to get there for the 8 o'clock bell. In winter they carried lanterns to find the way. During the day, these lanterns helped light the classroom. They also warmed hands and feet.

All grades, 1 to 8, learned from one teacher. Girls sat on one side of the room and boys on the other. If you were six, you learned your ABCs first. You sat with the teacher, then went to your bench to write on a black slate with a slate pencil. Older children read books and did arithmetic, usually "in their heads" without paper and pencil.

Modern-Day Visitors At Little Greenbrier School

You Learned Your ABCs First

Just for Fun

And what did people do for fun in those early days? Sometimes they were too busy to play. Besides, many people believed it was a sin to do anything but work.

They tried to have fun while they worked. Women gathered and talked as they made quilts. At harvest time there were corn-husking contests to see who could take husks off the most corn. Sorghum boiling was a time for fun and good eating.

Young people made their own toys out of stones and moss. Corn husks and sweet potatoes made good dolls. And sometimes a grandfather carved a dancing man called a Limber Jack.

People loved to gather for singing. Someone played a fiddle. Others played harmonicas or banjos, and everyone sang. Today the dulcimer, autoharp, and wooden recorder have been added to the music of the mountains.

When you visit, you may hear some of this "old timey" music. Ask about it at the Sugarlands Visitor Center.

Knock The Board So Limber Jack Will Dance

"Old Timey" Music With A Dulcimer

Recorder And Autoharp At Sugarlands Visitor Center

The Rangers

Wherever you go, Rangers give the park more meaning. Ranger-Historians tell the history of the mountains. Ranger-Naturalists explain the wonders of nature.

Day or night from May through October, you can enjoy programs about wildlife or how the pioneers lived. You can take a walk with a Ranger-Historian to visit an early settler's cabin. The Ranger explains how it was built and tells some of the tales the old-timers told. You can almost feel what it was like to build a home in this wilderness.

On nature walks Ranger-Naturalists tell about flowers, trees, and vines. You get to know which plants the mountain people used for medicine and what trees they used to build houses. A nature walk is a good time to learn what the poison ivy vine looks like.

Ask for a Visitor Program at Ranger Stations or Visitor Centers so you'll know when and where these programs are given.

Poison Ivy ►

Evergreens

Evergreen trees and shrubs stay green all year. Those with wide leaves are called broad-leaf evergreens. These include heath shrubs like mountain laurel and rhododendron.

Some evergreens called conifers have needles and bear their seeds in cones. Among the conifers in the park is the eastern hemlock. Along with other shade-loving trees like beech and maple, eastern hemlock trees fight for space to grow. Look on the trail at the Noah "Bud" Ogle Place Trail for eastern hemlocks with their short, shiny needles and tiny cones.

A visit to the Spruce-Fir Trail off Clingmans Dome Road is like a visit to a rain forest in Canada. Red spruce and Fraser fir grow here along with lichens, ferns, and moss.

Look at the cones to tell which is the spruce or fir. Spruce cones hang from the branches. The fir tree is the only conifer with upright cones. In fall the fir's upright cones come apart. Their parts scatter and leave spiked cores on the branches.

Lichens, Ferns, And Moss Grow In Shade Under Spruce And Fir ▶

Hardwood Forests

Great Smoky Mountains National Park has the biggest uncut hardwood forest in North America. At low elevations yellow poplar, basswood, sugar maple, and others grow in the coves. They're called cove hardwoods. Northern hardwoods, mainly American beech and yellow birch, grow above 4500 feet.

Why do the Smokies have so many trees? One reason is the rich soil; another is heavy rainfall. Also, some people think that millions of years ago, during the Ice Age, these mountains stood beyond the glaciers. They became a refuge, a safe place, where plants and animals could live. When the glaciers melted and the weather warmed, plants and animals spread back over the land.

Today, as a national park, the Smokies are still a refuge for plants and animals.

Every fall you can see how many different hardwoods there are when the trees turn red, yellow, brown, and orange.

Fall Colors Show How Many Hardwoods Grow Here ➤

Spring

Great Smoky Mountains National Park is open all year. In the spring, many visitors come to see the migrating birds on their way north for the summer.

More people come to see the many wildflowers. Before the trees have new leaves, the sun can shine on the hardwood forest floor. Sunlight and warmth bring about the seed sprouting of over 1500 different kinds of flowering plants. Crested dwarf iris and bluets show their tiny blue blossoms. Bees find the fringed phacelia, and yellow adder's tongue glows golden in the sun.

Every year during the last weekend in April, bus-loads of visitors come for the Wildflower Pilgrimage. During the pilgrimage there are morning and afternoon motor tours and guided walks. Early risers can take a morning bird walk before the flower walks. In the evening, flower experts give slide and movie programs about the wonders of this yearly rebirth in spring.

Crested Dwarf Iris

Fringed Phacelia

Yellow Adder's Tongue

Summer

Summer is good for camping, hiking, and fishing in the Smokies. It's also a good time to hike to the treeless mountain tops called "slicks" or "balds." How the balds were formed is a mystery.

Indian stories say the trees were cleared to make a lookout. They used the lookout to watch for "a monster who stole babies." But some people think wind or fire may have killed the trees or kept them from growing.

No matter how they were formed, balds are interesting places to see. Some are covered with grass, making them good places to look for different kinds of birds such as ravens and dark-eyed juncos.

Heath balds are covered with thick shrubs worth seeing. Two heaths that bloom in May and June are flame azalea and mountain laurel. An 11-mile hike to and from Gregory Bald takes you to the best display of flame azaleas in the park.

At the end of June, Andrews Bald is covered with rhododendrons in bloom. An easy two-mile hike to Andrews Bald starts near Clingmans Dome parking lot.

Rosebay Rhododendron ➤

Fall and Winter

In winter a few campers enjoy having the park almost to themselves. Sometimes they camp under a blanket of snow. But fall is almost as busy as spring and summer.

In fall the Smokies burst with color. You may wonder why trees turn so many different colors. A living leaf is green because of chlorophyll. Chlorophyll bodies in leaf cells make food for the plant. They use light, water, and a gas in the air called carbon dioxide to make food. Other colors, or pigments, in the leaf are covered by the green chlorophyll.

An October chill makes a layer form between the stem and twig. The leaf gets no more water and dies. The chlorophyll fades, and other pigments show through.

Orange and yellow leaves have carotin, the same pigment that makes carrots orange. Red and purple pigments are anthocyanins. Red maple, staghorn sumac, and dogwood leaves show their anthocyanins in the middle of October. Oak leaves are golden brown when tannin shows through the faded chlorophyll.

Red Maple

Maple, Magnolia, Birch, Oak, And Others

Staghorn Sumac

Flowering Dogwood

Black Oak

Camping and Fishing

You can stay outside the park in nearby towns where you find motels as well as campgrounds. Many people camp inside the park. With a tent or trailer, a "developed" campground may be your home away from home. These campgrounds have water, fireplaces, tables, benches, and public restrooms. They don't have shelters, showers, or electricity.

The "primitive" campgrounds have tables, fireplaces, and pit toilets.

People over 16 need a state fishing license from Tennessee or North Carolina, to fish in this park. Fishing goes on all year in streams called "open waters." You may fish from sunrise to sunset, but the limit is five of any kind of fish.

Ask a Park Ranger for the leaflets on camping and fishing. The fishing leaflet tells about closed and excluded waters, but a map shows where the open waters are. Rules on equipment say, "Use artificial flies or lures and only one hook."

May all your catches be over the size limit of seven inches for Trout and Bass (except Rock Bass on which there is no size limit).

Elkmont Campground ►

Hiking

There are more than 650 miles of trails in the Great Smoky Mountains National Park. Ask for the list of *WALKS AND HIKES* so you can choose from many places to walk or drive. Self-guiding trail maps explain what you see and make the trails more interesting. Will you walk a mile and a half to and from Juneywhank Falls, or eight miles to Mount Le Conte from Newfound Gap? Maybe you'll go up an easy 300 feet on a mile-and-a-quarter hike to Laurel Falls.

The longest marked trail in the world, the Appalachian Trail, runs from Maine to Georgia. Of its more than 2000 miles, 71 miles of this trail go the length of the Smokies.

National Park Service crews try to keep the famous Appalachian Trail in good shape. They put rocks and logs across the path to keep the waters of heavy rainfalls from rushing down the trail and making ruts. They also clear fallen trees.

If you camp in the backcountry, you need a free permit. When you get the permit, you tell where you plan to go and when you'll be back.

Even on a short hike, you need to wear a hat, carry water, and be ready for a change in weather.

Laurel Falls ►

Smokies - A Gift to Enjoy

Until June 15, 1934, the land for this park belonged to over 6000 farmers and lumber companies. Then how did the Smokies become a park?

It started in 1923 when Mr. and Mrs. W. P. Davis from Tennessee visited some national parks in the West. They thought the Smokies should become a national park.

But it would take over $10 million to buy all that land! The Davises started a group of people who felt as they did. Soon other groups joined in. They got cities to vote some of the money to buy the land. North Carolina and Tennessee gave money to the fund. Thousands of children gave nickels and dimes. By 1932, with only half of the money needed in the fund, many were ready to give up. But finally, Mr. John D. Rockefeller, Jr., gave a gift of $5 million in memory of his mother.

Today we have many people to thank for the Great Smoky Mountains National Park, a gift for all to enjoy.

The Author and Illustrator

Wyoming-born Ruth Radlauer's love affair with nature and national parks began in Wyoming where she spent her summers at camp on Casper Mountain or traveling with her family in Yellowstone National Park.

Mr. and Mrs. Radlauer, graduates of the University of California at Los Angeles, are authors of many books for young people of all ages. Their subjects range from robots to radio and volcanoes to coral reefs.

Photographing the national parks is a labor of love for Rolf Zillmer and his wife Evelyn. The Zillmers get an intimate view of each park, since they are backpack and wildlife enthusiasts.

A former student at Art Center College of Design in Los Angeles, Mr. Zillmer is a fine sculptor of wildlife cast in bronze. He was born in New York City and now makes his home in California where he is the Art Director for Elk Grove Books.